THE BEST OF
HARVEY PENICK'S
LITTLE GREEN
GOLF BOOK

HARVEY PENICK
WITH BUD SHRAKE

D0993332

CollinsWillow
An Imprint of HarperCollinsPublishers

This edition published in 1996 for
Emap Pursuit Publishing Ltd by
HarperCollins*Publishers*
77-85 Fulham Palace Road
Hammersmith, London W6 8JB

Published in 1994 by Collins Willow
an imprint of HarperCollins*Publishers*
Reprinted 1994,1995 (twice)
First published in 1993 by Simon & Schuster

ISBN 0583 32450-9

Printed and bound in Great Britain

What Does It Mean?

EVER SINCE Ben Hogan's book, *Five Lessons: The Modern Fundamentals of Golf*, was published in 1957, hardly a week has gone by without at least one pupil wanting to engage me in a discussion about "pronation" and "supination."

Usually it begins with the pupil asking, "What do 'pronation' and 'supination' really mean, anyhow?"

The actions indicated by those words have been a natural part of the golf swing since the game began. Seymour Dunn, a Scot from North Berwick, wrote what he called a "scientific explanation" of pronation and supination in a book published in 1922. My son, Tinsley, and I used to study the photographs in Dunn's book when Tinsley was a boy.

But the average golfer had never given a conscious thought to pronation and supination until Hogan's book—written by Herbert Warren Wind and illustrated by Anthony Ravielli—captured the public fancy.

I stay away from those words in my teaching.

But to answer the question of what they really mean, as simply as possible, this is what I say:

"My dictionary says pronation is turning the hand so the palm faces downward. Supination is turning the hand so the palm faces upward. Now forget about those words, and let's get back to golf."

Take Pleasure in It

I WAS INVITED to be honorary starter at the Texas Women's Amateur championship when it was played at the Barton Creek Club. It was a thrill to be wanted by so many women.

As the first morning matches were setting off, one of my Austin Country Club friends and pupils, Carrell Grigsby, came over and knelt beside my golf cart and held my hand.

I could feel in her grip, and see in her eyes, that Carrell was nervous.

I sent her soothing thoughts, but we didn't talk much. There were other players needing attention.

Carrel squeezed my hand and stood up.

"Well, Harvey," she said, clearing her throat. "I have to go play now."

I caught her hand and pulled her back.

"Carrell," I said. "You don't *have* to go play. You *get* to go play. There's a world of difference."

A sudden grin lit the worry off her face.

"You're right," she said. "What am I scared of? This is fun!"

I wish I could say Carrell won the tournament. For sure I can report that she received great pleasure from playing in it. Never again have I heard her say she *has* to play golf.

Playing golf is a privilege, not a sentence.

Flavor That Lasts

IF YOU WERE asked to imagine what flavor of ice cream would describe your golf swing, I would like to hear you answer, "vanilla."

The more simple your approach to the swing is, the better off you are. It's the simple things that last.

The Oracle Speaks

HARRIS GREENWOOD, A college player of mine who later became a lawyer in Houston, filled me in on the background of this story long after it happened.

The way Harris told it, there was a young golfer in his Houston crowd who was their equal or better in daily games. This fellow would win money from them, but in the weekend tournaments, his scores were inexplicably high. Rather than winning the weekend tournaments, as this fellow had the talent to do, he finished in the middle of the pack.

Harris had always come to me for lessons, as had several others in that Houston bunch. They started telling this fellow, "Harvey can solve all your problems. If you can just spend a little time with Harvey, he will heal you. Harvey will touch your clubs and give you his blessing, and all will be okay."

I didn't know this was going on, of course. When Harris phoned me to arrange a lesson for this fellow, he just told me his friend needed help.

He scheduled the lesson for five weeks in advance. Harris and his friends wanted the time to continue fooling with this fellow's mind. They counted down the days. They told him, "Harvey is the high priest of golf. He will do magic. The rest of us will never be in the winner's circle again. You will become a dominant force in amateur golf after you visit Harvey."

The night before the lesson, this fellow drove to Austin. He spent the night at the Terrace Motel and went to bed early.

Now I enter the story.

It is barely daylight, and I am in the golf shop at Austin Country Club. This young fellow comes in and introduces himself as my pupil from Houston. I tell him to take a couple of buckets of balls and go warm up.

Later I wander out to the practice tee and watch him. I am surprised. This fellow hits it like a pro. I don't say a word. I rest my chin in my hand and stand behind him, stand at every angle, watching in admiration as this fellow hits shot after shot as crisply as you please.

For a whole hour this fellow hits balls. I don't say a word except to tell him when to switch to a different club.

At last it is time for me to say something.

I can tell by the anxious way he bites his lip that he is expecting to hear a decree from an oracle.

"Well, son," I say. "You line up to the ball real well. You have a good strong grip that I like. You stay down and behind the ball well. You hit it solid. Would you mind telling me what were your last two scores?"

"I played in a tournament last weekend," he says. "I shot a 77 on Saturday and would have had about 78 on Sunday, except I put the ball in my pocket."

"There's only one thing I see wrong with your game," I say.

"What is it?" he cries.

"Your scores are too high," I say.

This fellow is speechless. Then he becomes irate.

"Is that all?" he says.

"That's all I can see."

He takes his clubs over to his car, slams the trunk shut, slams the driver's door, and roars off on his way back to Houston.

Now I leave the story again, so far as I know.

Back in Houston—Harris told me later—this fellow at first wouldn't tell them about his lesson. They kept pushing him for details. They pushed until he blew up. "That Harvey Penick is a fraud!" he yelled. "He doesn't know anything about golf! He didn't give me a single bit of instruction that will help my swing! He just told me I ought to shoot better scores! I didn't need to drive all the way to Austin to have some old fool tell me my scores are too high!"

The next weekend this young fellow went out and won his first golf tournament.

Apparently all he needed was to be told it was all right for him to do it.

A Story by Helen

THE TELEPHONE RINGS frequently in the kitchen of our home near Austin Country Club.

Unless one of Harvey's day nurses get the phone while I'm shopping or playing cards—I love bridge and gin rummy—I'm the one who answers.

Harvey sits in his favorite chair in the living room beyond the open kitchen door. He is about twenty feet from the phone. But Harvey hasn't been able to walk for several years now, and his hearing is poor. It is a terrible strain for him to try to talk on the phone.

As a result, I have become the translator between Harvey and his callers.

You can't believe some of the calls I have answered.

I have given putting lessons to golf pros on the phone, shouting their questions to Harvey.

All sorts of people phone Harvey, from golf pros to average players to fans and friends and those who are just plain curious.

Recently I picked up the phone and heard a man say, "Put Harvey Penick on the line, please."

I explained about Harvey's problem with the phone.

"Well, you tell him I am coming to see him for a week of lessons," the man said.

"I don't know if Harvey will be able to see you," I said. "Especially not for a whole week. It's a bit too hard on him."

"What's hard about it?"

I said, "Harvey is getting along in years, you know."

"He is, is he?" the man said. "You tell him to fire up and get ready to teach. I'm leaving in a few minutes, driving down there from Sacramento."

I said, "I'm afraid you are wasting your time."

The man said, "Nope, I have no time to waste. You see, I am ninety years old myself."

I'm sure Harvey will see him, but the man hasn't arrived. I hope his time didn't run out while he was on his way.

Another Call

I HEARD THE PHONE RING, and moments later Helen appeared in the kitchen doorway.

"Harvey, this is a woman calling from Providence, Rhode Island. Her name is Paula Granoff. She says she has played golf for years but had never won anything until she read your *Little Red Book*. Right after she read it, she won the Rhode Island Senior Amateur."

"Tell her, congratulations on her good playing," I said.

Helen spoke on the phone again. Then she returned to the door.

"She wants to come to Austin and take lessons," Helen said.

"If she just won the state championship, what does she need with lessons?" I said.

After another phone conversation, Helen came all the way into the living room and stood beside my chair.

"Harvey, she says she wants to come to Texas to meet the great teacher," Helen said. "I wonder who on earth she has in mind?"

Toss It

ONE AFTERNOON, I was standing at the edge of the putting green with Ben Crenshaw and his good friend Billy Munn, who had been captain of one of my university golf teams and my number-one player.

Billy had talked to me about turning pro when his college career ended. But this was in the early sixties. Billy's hometown, Midland, was rich with oil money, and the pro golf tour paid off in peanuts, compared to the winning purses of today. A young man of means in Midland in Billy's day was expected to take up a career as a banker, doctor, lawyer, or oil man—not as a golf pro.

He had asked me what he should do. This was Billy's whole life we were talking about. I certainly didn't want to tell him the wrong thing. All I said to him was, "Billy, whichever career you choose will not give you integrity. You have to bring integrity with you."

Billy chose the oil business—partly because he'd had four knee operations and wasn't sure he could stand up to the physical grind of the tour.

This day, on the edge of the putting green with Billy and Ben, we were discussing what club to use to chip the ball to a hole near the outside of the green.

"Ben, you're a good athlete," I said. "Pick up a ball and toss it underhand close to that hole."

The ball rolled to within a foot of the cup.

"You tossed that ball real low," I said. "Why didn't you throw it high up in the air, like it would have gone if you had been using an open-face wedge?"

"Because you said to get it close," Ben said.

"Exactly," I said. "What club would produce the same flight and result of that underhand toss you just made? Whatever club you think would do it, that's the club to choose."

An Irony

IN GOLF YOUR strengths and weaknesses will always be there. If you could improve your weaknesses, you would improve your game.

The irony is that people prefer to practice their strengths.

The First Choice

WHEN YOU ARE TRYING to decide which club to hit, the first one that comes to mind is the right one.

Let us suppose your instinct tells you to pull a 5-iron out of the bag.

Your instinct is correct. Hit the 5-iron.

But you throw up some grass to test the wind and you check the yardage again, and you overrule your instinct. You change to a 4-iron, or maybe to a 6-iron.

Now you are no longer sure. You'll probably ease up on the 4-iron or really bear down on the 6-iron. The result is liable to be a poor shot.

Go ahead and hit the club your inner voice first tells you to hit. If your judgment is a little off, so what? It's only a few yards' difference between clubs.

The important difference is in confidence.

Confidence is contagious.

A Strange World

CALL ME OLD-FASHIONED or starchy or whatever you will, but two things in this world I just can't grow accustomed to are a man and a woman living together without being married—and taking a mulligan at golf.

Look Here First

NINE OUT OF TEN problems with the swing of the average golfer begin with the grip or the stance.

The symptoms that come from these two sources are many and various.

It is easy for teachers to get caught up in treating the symptoms without first going to the underlying causes in the grip and the stance.

Toward a Stronger Grip

FOR A NUMBER of years during Ben Hogan's prime and thereafter, many golf teachers taught the neutral grip—in which the V's of the thumbs and forefingers point more or less toward the nose or right eye.

This was Hogan's grip, and it was the right thing for him because he was always fighting a hook. In fact, most good players tend to be hookers. This neutral grip worked well for the good players and still does.

For players who are not so good, the neutral grip encourages a slice.

Recently, some gentlemen from Tokyo came to visit with me at Austin Country Club. We were sitting in the grassy patio, nibbling at hors d'ouevres from a tray, drinking iced tea, and chatting about golf through an interpreter.

Mr. Tsuyoshi Honjo, editor in chief of *Baffy* magazine, asked if I would look at his grip. He removed his jacket, rolled up his sleeves, and placed his hands on a 7-iron that was sent out from the golf shop.

His V's pointed straight at his nose.

"I see you have read Ben Hogan's book," I said.

"Oh yes, oh yes," he beamed. "Everyone has read Mr. Hogan's book."

"I imagine you are quite a slicer," I said.

"Oh yes, oh yes," he said, not so happily. "Very big slice."

I asked him to roll both his hands to the right until his V's pointed at his right shoulder. I tossed a little tiny carrot off the tray, into the grass at his feet.

"Hit that carrot," I said.

We kept it up for half an hour, Mr. Tsuyoshi Honjo hitting tiny carrots off the patio grass with a 7-iron and a strong grip.

The reason I wanted him to hit the carrots instead of golf balls is that he would have no expectation about hitting carrots, and so his mind would be free to concentrate on the grip and the swing. If we had put a golf ball in front of him, he would probably get tense. (Later I told Tommy Kite about this. He grinned and said, "You have a new saying now—clip the carrot.")

"How does that grip feel?" I asked my Japanese visitor.

"I think I hit it much harder and farther." He smiled.

"Please practice that grip and that swing, hitting carrots or leaves or twigs, until you feel good about it," I said. "Then go to the practice range and use the grip and swing on some golf balls. I think you will be pleased."

The Japanese gentlemen were quite excited when they left the patio on their way to pay a call on Columbia Lakes, near Houston, where Kathy Whitworth, Betsy Cullen, and Mark Steinbauer are teaching.

In the last few years I have noticed that the golf grip is evolving back toward a stronger position. In the days of Vardon, the V's pointed at the right shoulder. During the era of Hogan, the V's moved to point at the nose. Now, in the days of Freddie Couples, Davis Love III, John Daly, and others, the grip has once again moved the V's toward the right shoulder.

I believe this is because of all the good modern players who have learned to combine the hands-and-arms swing of the strong grip with the big muscle swing of the neutral grip.

Without a doubt, the strong grip is better for the average player. As Mr. Tsuyoshi Honjo said, a less-than-expert player soon feels he can hit the ball harder and farther with a strong grip.

But like any other golf teaching, a strong grip can be overdone.

Kathy, Betsy, and Mark teach, among others, groups of young Japanese women who are selected to come to Columbia Lakes to train to be golf professionals.

They brought some of their Japanese pupils to see me at the practice area at Austin Country Club. The girls were each told to hit a few 5-irons for me. One girl in particular really gave that ball a smack.

"What do you think of her?" Kathy said.

"I think she can't hit a driver," I said.

The young Japanese understood me. She smiled and pulled out of her pocket a tee four inches long. That's how high she had to tee it up to use her driver.

It was all in her grip. This girl's grip was four-knuckles, V's pointed to the right of the right shoulder, like an old West-Texas grip. With that grip, she de-lofted the club so much that it took a four-inch tee for her driver to reach the ball.

"Let me see your golf club," I said.

The Japanese girl ducked her head bashfully and handed me the club. As I had suspected, it was not a 5-iron. It was a 7-iron. Her grip was turning it into a 4-iron.

She had learned that grip at home, I must point out—not at Columbia Lakes.

All You Need to Know About the Wrist Cock

So MUCH HAS BEEN WRITTEN and spoken about it that the wrist cock has become a literature of its own.

Let's keep it simple.

Take your stance. Swing your club back to waist high. If the toe of your club is pointing straight up, the wrist cock is built into your swing. Think no more about it.

To see the wrist cock in your living room without a

golf club, just take your stance. Let your left arm hang down and put your right arm behind your back to get it out of the way.

Make your left hand like a blade, the back of the hand facing your imaginary target down the line. Swing your left arm back to the top of your backswing and stop.

Clench your left hand into a fist.

Your wrist is cocked. Now you know how it feels.

Another way to get the feeling of a cocked wrist is to swing your left fist all the way through as if it were holding a golf club.

That's all you need. I would prefer that you delve no further into the literature of the wrist cock.

Higher Aspects

PEOPLE SAY TO ME that golf is a *spiritual* game. I don't believe I understand how that word applies to golf. According to my dictionary, the first meaning of *spiritual* is "Of the spirit or the soul as distinguished from the body."

It is true that golf is a game in which you seem to get in touch with higher parts of yourself. We can say golf is spiritual in that respect. But we can't leave the body out of the golf swing, can we?

All my life I have been asking people what the difference is between faith and confidence.

One of my pupils told me, "Confidence is that feeling I get just before I learn better."

Another said, "Confidence in golf is when I am faced with a certain shot that I have hit successfully many times, and I know full well I will do it again. Faith is when I may never have hit this particular shot before, but I trust that I can do it because I have faith in my swing."

Most people say faith is religious, but they feel that confidence is something different.

My dictionary says faith is "Unquestioning belief in God, religion, or a system of religious beliefs."

Confidence, according to my dictionary, is "Firm belief in the truth or reality of a fact, or trust and reliance on one's own abilities."

It seems to me that confidence is the feeling we want to have in playing golf. But we can't dismiss the value of faith, either.

I think faith is in the heart, and confidence is in the mind.

A Method for Madness

A FRIEND WROTE me a letter from Sawgrass Country Club in Ponte Vedra, Florida.

He wanted to know, "How can I keep from getting so insanely mad on the golf course? I know losing my temper is not good for my game. But when I blow a short putt and then hook a drive into the marsh, I go crazy with anger and despair. Then things get rapidly worse. I know it's stupid to get mad but what can I do?"

I think it is fine to get mad if you hit a poor shot or miss a putt you should have made. Getting mad shows you have the competitive spirit. They call him "Gentle Ben" Crenshaw, but he's always had flashes of temper on the course because he wants to win and he wants to be the best.

So get mad. But do it in a gentlemanly way.

In your mind call yourself every name you can think of for the poor shot you just hit.

But while you are being mad, be mad only at yourself.

Do not be mad at your clubs or the golf course. They're the same as they were when you hit a great shot yesterday. And don't be mad at luck. Stick to the one thing you can control: you.

Then forget it. Cast the bad names out of your mind and be thinking positively by the time you approach your next shot. Your next shot is a new experience. It might be the best shot you ever hit in your life.

Making a Comeback

EVERY TEACHER IS familiar with this pupil.

He is about fifty years old. He was a good player as a youth and was a long hitter off the tee. A person's memory tends to add a good many yards to his youthful tee shots. But this pupil I am describing really was a long hitter and had some success in amateur tournaments.

After college he went into a business or a profession and did well at it. He kept playing golf through his twenties. Gradually he began to play only on weekends. The demands of family and his striving to be good at his chosen calling eventually left him with no time for golf.

At about age thirty he was playing maybe three or four times a year at charity events or conventions. His scores climbed into the 90s. He was embarrassed to play poorly. He remembered what a joy the game had been when he was near scratch. Those days, he decided, were gone forever.

He packed his clubs in the closet and gave it up.

Twenty years later, his kids have left the nest, his wife is busy with volunteer work, his finances look pretty comfortable, and he finds he has increasing free time. His thoughts drift back to golf.

He arranges for a lesson.

The first morning on the practice range, after we get to know each other a little, I ask why he has driven all the way from Dallas to take a lesson from me at Austin Country Club.

He admits he had a lesson from another teacher the previous week, but he wasn't satisfied. He starts to show me what the other teacher had told him.

"If you don't mind," I say, cutting him off politely, "I had rather not hear what someone else told you. Please hit a few balls with your 7-iron, and I will watch."

He says, "Pro, my big problem is my loss of distance. I've been hitting balls on my own for a couple of months. I get worse and worse. The more balls I hit, the shorter they go. I don't understand it. I lift weights, I use hand-grippers daily, and I jog three miles every morning. I'm in the best shape I've been in since I was twenty-five years old. And yet I've lost all my distance."

His mention of lifting weights is a red flag.

I strongly believe in physical conditioning. In my opinion, the main reason the modern touring pros hit the ball so far is that they are stronger and in better shape than the pros of early days. But a golfer must be extremely careful about weight lifting. He may strengthen the wrong muscles and hurt his swing instead of helping it.

"Let's leave distance for later," I tell this pupil. "See

that flag near that small stone wall about 150 yards down there? Hit a ball to that flag for me."

He hits several shots. I don't watch the ball. I watch his swing.

"You are aiming west and trying to hit north," I tell him.

"I'm aiming a little to the left so I can hit out on the ball," he says.

"Lee Trevino can aim west and hit north, because he lets his head drop down half a foot as he hits the ball. I want you to stand up taller and aim square to the hole. Or even aim a little to the right of the hole and play a right-to-left shot."

I back up my golf cart and turn it to point straight at the flag. I ask him to square up his stance to my cart and hit balls directly at the target.

He makes a few more swings. I stop him.

"I'm going to tell you something you are not going to like," I say. "If you are not going to follow my advice, we are both wasting our time. You're like most Dallas people—always in a hurry. Dallas people do everything like they are working by the job. I want you to work by the hour."

He swiftly rakes over another ball to hit, but I stop him again.

"I'm not going to tell you a negative thing, like not to swing so hard, and I'm not going to tell you to swing slow," I say. "Just swing like you're doing it by the hour. There's no rush."

I ask him to put the ball on a low tee.

"Now," I say. "Work by the hour and cut off that tee, and I will show you a good shot."

Swing after swing, over and over, I repeat the instructions.

"You know," I say at last, "sitting here telling you the same thing over and over again doesn't make either of us look very bright. If you want your distance back, you'll do it by hitting the ball solid, not by hitting it fast. You're going to have to learn to work by the hour and cut off the tee to get your distance back."

The magical word "distance" persuades him to try to do as I ask. He hits a few good ones. He grins. He hits a bad one. I notice he changes his grip.

"Don't worry about making an adjustment every time you hit a bad shot," I say. "Never make a change based on one shot, or even a few shots. Wait for a pattern to develop."

He says he has taken up wearing glasses since his glorious youth, and perhaps he does not see the ball so well.

I tell him Jimmy Demaret used to throw down three or four balls on the tee during a practice round and hit each of them perfectly while looking at the gallery and telling jokes.

"If your swing is grooved, you can hit the ball with a sack over your head," I say. "Let's keep on clipping off that tee and working by the hour."

At last he understands that I have told him all I am going to tell him by way of instruction in this lesson, and if he doesn't clip off the tee and work by the hour, it has been a fruitless trip from Dallas.

When the realization sinks in, he begins hitting the ball solidly. I put a 3-wood in his hands. He hits the ball far and with a right-to-left tail on it.

He is thrilled. My arms tingle with pleasure.

"One more thing," I say as the lesson is ending. "Promise me you won't reach for your driver until you are able to hit the fairway ten times out of ten with your 3-wood."

"Thanks, Pro," he says. "I'll keep practicing, and maybe I'll try to qualify for the National Amateur next summer. Do you think I have a chance?"

"Sure you have a chance," I say. "If you can putt."

A Distinction

THE ABILITY to concentrate is good, but thinking too much about how you are doing what you are doing is disastrous.

Trust your muscles and hit the ball to the hole. Keep it simple.

Preacher Mann

THE FIRST TIME Dr. Gerald Mann, pastor of the River-bend Baptist Church, came to me for a golf lesson, we started in the customary way with him hitting a 7-iron and trying to clip off the tee.

He hit a hook and I said, "I don't believe it. Hit another."

Again he hit a hook. I asked him to hit several more balls, and all were hooks.

He said, "Why are you looking at me like that?"

"I still don't believe what I am seeing, and I thought I had seen every kind of golf swing there is. Everything about your grip, address, and swing tells me you should be shanking the ball. But you're hooking it. You have a God-given athletic ability."

We ended that first lesson on the positive thought that Dr. Mann was blessed with athletic ability. It was a long while before he came back to let me help him with the fundamentals.

I have played a lot of golf with preachers. One minister I recall would, after missing a short putt, turn to another member of the group and ask, "Would you mind expressing aloud my sentiments about that?"

As anyone who has played with him will tell you, Gerald Mann is not at all reluctant to express his sentiments.

Tom and Christy Kite and their kids attend the River-bend Baptist Church.

On the Sunday in the summer of 1992 when Tommy was about to tee off for the final round of the U.S. Open at Pebble Beach, Dr. Mann told his congregation:

"I don't know if God is into golf. But I am praying for Tom Kite to win the Open, and I want you to pray for him, too. If you don't want to pray for Tommy, I suggest you go someplace where they don't pray for winners."

The Reason for It

I HAVE ALWAYS TRIED to impress on my members and my pupils that the rules of golf are made to protect you, not for you to gain by them.

From the Fringe

ON A PAR FOUR, if your ball is on the fringe of the green in two strokes and you require three more strokes to get into the hole, you might as well have whiffed your tee shot.

The penalty is the same—the loss of one stroke.

If you whiffed your tee shot, you would be embarrassed. But if you take three from the fringe, you are apt to say, "Well, that's just my game."

You should feel that you can get down in two from the fringe every time. Practice it. There's no use throwing away all those strokes.

South of the Border

GOLF TEACHER CHUCK COOK tells the story that shortly after World War II a promising young player in Los Angeles asked noted amateur Wilford Wehrle for a lesson.

Wehrle broke open a sleeve of brand-new Spalding

balls and tossed one onto the ground at the youngster's feet.

"Let's see you hit it," Wehrle said.

Already nervous to be in Wehrle's company, the young player now was thoroughly frightened. He had never even seen a brand-new golf ball before. During the war, new golf balls scarcely ever entered a civilian's hands.

The youngster made a swing, caught the ball thin, and cut a horrible gash in it.

Wehrle muttered an oath and tossed another new Spalding onto the grass.

"Try it again," he said.

The trembling youngster topped the ball and nearly cut it in half.

Disgusted, Wehrle grabbed the iron club out of the youngster's hand and began swinging it into the ground, tearing up big chunks of earth.

In his anger Wehrle chopped a dozen huge divots.

"Son," he yelled, "the first thing you've got to learn is that golf is a game of digging holes!"

It is, of course, true that one of the paradoxes of golf is that you must hit down on the ball to make it rise.

A most common fault with beginners—and with poor players who have struggled for years—is trying to help the ball into the air by hitting it on the upswing with an iron club.

Until you learn to hit down and through the ball, you cannot play a decent iron shot.

However, I am not a believer in digging big divots. I believe it is better to pick the ball off the grass than to hoe it.

There are great players, I know, who whack out divots

the size of pie pans. But what I like to see is a shallow divot that is shaped like a dollar bill, the sort of divot Byron Nelson produced.

This reminds me of a teaching job I had at the Club Compestre in Monterrey, Mexico.

The person who hired me said, "Harvey, can you spare a couple of weeks to come give lessons at our club? We really need help."

"What is the problem?" I asked.

He said, "Our whole club is full of shankers."

In the autumn, I flew down to Monterrey. Sure enough, it was a club full of shankers. I hate to use that word—a "lateral shot" sounds nicer—because it conjures up one of the ugliest sights in golf.

But there was no getting around it.

This club was infested with shankers, as if they all had a disease.

It didn't take me long to discover the reason.

The club's regular teaching pro—who was away on vacation—had one firm principle that he drummed into his pupils. He told them, "Hit down, hit down, hit down, and hit down!"

Golf, for him, was truly a game of digging holes.

The danger in hitting down on the ball with such intensity is that you are likely to shank it.

If you are going to play golf by digging holes, you must have a good, fast hip turn and hit through the ball, or you can expect to foul it into the dugout.

I spent a couple of pleasant weeks in the brisk mountain climate of Monterrey, teaching the club members that there is more to golf than digging holes.

I believe it is impossible to shank a ball with a closed

blade. It was a joy to see their happiness when their shank went away.

When it was time for me to return to Austin, they paid me off in cash—a fat roll of big, very colorful bills.

I had never seen that much money. I don't remember now how much it translated to back in Texas, but it made me about half nervous to have so much cash. I stretched rubber bands around the roll and then tied a piece of string around it, stuffed the money into my pocket and tied the string to my belt loop.

Sitting on the plane, waiting to take off, the fellow next to me leaned over and said, "Excuse me. Isn't your name Harvey?"

I said yes.

He said, "They're paging you. They want you back inside the airport."

I thought, oh my gosh, they've come to their senses and realized they paid me way too much. I'm going to have to march right in there and give this big roll of money back to them.

But that wasn't it at all. It was just some minor thing with the luggage. I got back home with the whole roll.

And you know what? The next autumn, they hired me to come back to the same club for another two weeks of teaching.

Their regular pro had returned after I left, and started drilling them again to hit down, hit down, and hit down.

They all started shanking again.

The Lay Up

ONE OF THE WORST SHOTS in golf is when a player de-
cides to lay up short of a hazard and yet hits enough club
to reach the trouble—and usually does.

Often this is because the player chooses a club that will
land close as possible short of the hazard. He hits it easy,
he thinks. But his easy swing catches the ball solid and it
goes ten yards farther than usual.

If you are laying up, be sure you lay up and not in.

You might think of the shot as "laying back" from the
hazard, rather than "laying up" to the edge of it.

Tommy Wins
the Open

ON THE FINAL DAY of the 1992 U.S. Open at Pebble
Beach, with the wind and rain howling in off the ocean,
Tommy Kite played one of the finest, most courageous
rounds of golf in the history of the game.

Sitting in front of my television back home in Austin,

I was so moved and so proud of Tommy that my toes curled up and I cried like a baby when they put the championship trophy in his hands at the end of that excruciating day.

When Tommy came by to visit with me sometime later, I asked what he had been thinking about during the hours he was battling horrible weather conditions to emerge as champion over the best players in the world.

I have always impressed on my pupils that when they're playing in the wind and rain and cold, they should take their time. I don't mean play slow. I mean just don't hurry.

So it warmed my heart when Tommy said, "I was thinking, 'Take your time.'"

I asked him to tell me about it.

"In a situation like that," he said, "with players being blown away, somehow you've got to forget about your swing or any mechanical thoughts and get into a really trusting mentality.

"You just have to take the attitude that you have done all the training that is required, and if you're not going to trust it, why do all the training?"

He got that line from sports psychologist Dr. Bob Rotella. I love that line. Trust it.

"I use that thought an awful lot when I'm on the golf course and have a chance to win the tournament," Tommy said. "I keep telling myself to trust it, just go ahead and trust it.

"There's no point in training and working hard if when you get out there on the golf course or the football field or whatever, you're not going to trust the fact that you know how to do it. Like Troy Aikman. He trusts himself to throw the football where he wants to put it. Otherwise, why should he bother with all that practice?

"As for taking my time, I mean I want to be totally ready to play the shot before I play the shot. I must be 100 percent committed to playing this particular shot at this particular moment. In bad weather, if it takes a little longer to get ready, then I need to take a little longer."

We remembered one year at the Masters when Ben Crenshaw was preparing to hit his approach shot to the 72nd hole. Ben needed a birdie to win his second Masters or a par to get into a playoff. It was raining. Ben's glove was wet. He missed the green, made a bogey on the hole, and finished second.

"Ben just got into a little bit of a rush," Tommy said. "It would only have taken a minute for him to reach in his bag and pull out a brand-new dry glove right out of a package and feel good about it.

"It was kind of like he was thinking, well, you know, it's okay, I can hit this shot anyway. And then when you miss it, you're kicking yourself in the rear all the way.

"Lee Trevino made the comment, 'I don't care if you have to send your caddie into the pro shop to buy a new glove. When you've got the Masters laying on the line, you don't hit the ball until you are ready.' I'm not picking on Ben when I say this, because I've done dumb things like that way too often.

"When I woke up Sunday morning at the Open and stepped outside and felt the wind and rain in my face, I knew I had an excellent chance to win if I just took my time and trusted myself."

Tommy took dead aim that day.

A Story by
Christy Kite

AFTER TOM WON THE Open on Sunday, he was supposed to play an outing in St. Louis the next day. Monterey, California, is not the easiest place in the world to get out of, so I decided I would fly to St. Louis with him and then fly home to Austin on Monday morning rather than spending the night by myself in Monterey.

They had two private planes waiting to take us to St. Louis. Most people took the earlier one. The only people on the later plane were Craig Stadler and us.

The plane was delayed, so Craig went to dinner. We were waiting for him to come back. Now it was just Tom and I on the plane, and we had the U.S. Open Trophy with us.

Tom said, "You'll be flying home tomorrow, but the first thing Tuesday morning, I want you to take this trophy over to Mr. Penick and set it right in his lap."

Tuesday morning, I took the trophy to Austin Country Club, where Mr. Penick was giving a lesson to a woman who had come down from Rhode Island to see him.

I walked up to his golf cart and said, "Mr. Penick, this is for you."

I put the U.S. Open Trophy in his lap.

I said, "Tom said a big piece of this trophy belongs to you."

Mr. Penick started crying. I started crying. Pretty soon all the people around his cart were crying and laughing at the same time.

I wish Tom could have been there to give Mr. Penick the trophy himself, but he couldn't, and I did it the way Tom wanted me to do it. It was a great pleasure, that's for sure.

Make Up Your Mind

ON EVERY KIND of golf shot, you must make up your mind exactly what it is you want to do. Do not have the slightest doubt. As a friend of mine says of the way he lives his life, "I may be wrong, but I am never in doubt."

If there is doubt in your mind over a golf shot, how can your muscles know what they are expected to do?

What most average players can't seem to grasp is that this is just as true of a two-foot putt as it is of any other shot.

Watching the Bob Hope Tournament on television one Saturday, I saw Tommy Kite coming down the stretch miss a putt that was so short, he could easily have kicked it in.

The television commentator said Tommy's stroke

broke down. Well, I could see that it wasn't a great stroke, but I doubted if mechanics had anything to do with missing the putt.

On Sunday, Tommy holed everything he looked at, shot a course record, and won the tournament going away at 35 under par.

When he came home, I asked him about that putt he missed on Saturday.

"I'd had the same putt in a practice round," he said. "The green back there has so much slope to it that it looks like it breaks off the world. When I stood over the putt in the tournament, I was thinking it was just outside the right edge of the hole. But I looked again and thought, whoa, I'm playing too much break. I know it breaks a lot, but, gosh, does it break this much?

"Instead of stepping back and starting over with a clear mind, I stroked the putt and missed it. Missing the putt had nothing to do with the stroke. I missed it because I wasn't thinking right. I wasn't ready to play the shot.

"Sunday I knew I was going to putt well. All I did was make up my mind I would be totally committed to every stroke."

If this is what is required of the U.S. Open champion, how can the average golfer expect to get by with less?

The California
Woman

I WAS GIVING a lesson to a woman from California who
already had a pretty good game, but wanted to lower her
handicap to a single number.

Something was wrong.

She was hitting the ball decently, but she kept frown-
ing and fidgeting.

After half an hour she said, "Harvey, what you are
telling me is too simple. It is so simple that I can't understand it."

It wasn't the first time I have been criticized for being
too simple, nor was it the last.

Some pupils are not happy unless the teacher gives
them plenty of technical talk to chew on. They want the
teacher to fill their minds with "golf-swing theory."

These pupils leave me and move on to other, smarter
teachers.

No hard feelings on my part.

From my point of view, I don't teach theory. I teach
simple things that produce good results.

The woman from California said, "I don't understand
what you mean by 'clip off the tee.' "

"But you've been doing it," I said. "Are you unhappy with the results?"

"No, the results are fine. What I want to know is *why* the results are fine."

"Because when you clip off the tee you square your clubface," I said.

"I know that," she said. "But *why* does it square my clubface?"

"It's natural," I said.

"That's not a good enough answer," she said.

A few days earlier, the touring pro Tommy Aaron had come to the club for a lesson. I watched him hit balls all afternoon. At the end he said, "Well, what's the answer?"

I said, "You hit the ball beautifully. Ball-striking is not the reason you aren't winning."

"So what is the reason?" he asked.

"I don't know," I said.

That was not the answer Tommy wanted, but it was honest.

The woman from California stuck her club back in the bag, peeled off her glove, and said, "You make it sound too easy. My husband is the one you ought to be teaching. He's dumb enough to understand you. What do I owe you for this lesson?"

"Nothing," I said.

"You can't mean that."

"How could I charge you money for not helping you?" I said.

"But this is embarrassing. I must pay you for your time."

She left angry that I wouldn't take her money. There's no pleasing some people.

The Judge

HE WAS A JUDGE from out of town.

His overlapping stomach presented the judge with a dilemma. If he stood where he could see the ball, he couldn't reach it. If he stood where he could hit the ball, he couldn't see it.

After five lessons in a week, I had done very little to improve the judge's golf swing. But he was preparing to return home, and I wanted to give him at least one positive thought.

"Judge," I said, "I have a suggestion that will help make your game more fun."

"What is it?" he asked.

"Always play with clean golf balls."

Keep It Moving

POOR PLAYERS USUALLY seem embarrassed to play with good players.

The fact is that you may not be good enough to play with the good players, but no one will notice if you keep up.

The good players are not going to be watching you and criticizing your swing. They have their own games to deal with.

But if you hold up play, the others will notice you— and probably not in a kindly manner.

If you, as a poor player, lose your temper along with your golf balls, and shout and throw clubs and curse your luck, and plumb-bob all your putts from both sides of the hole, the good players will be disgusted. They'll avoid you for the rest of your life, not only on the golf course, but in the social and business worlds as well.

So just keep the game moving in a good humor, and you will always be welcome.

The Learning Game

A WOMAN FROM BOSTON wrote a letter asking if I would help her husband with his putting.

Her husband, she said, is a senior and a good player. His usual score is about 75. But lately his putting has gone sour. So sour, in fact, that it was making him hard to live with.

"Could he come to Austin and take a couple of lessons from you to straighten out his stroke?" she wrote.

In my opinion, I told her, the best thing her husband could do would be to stay right there in Boston and take up playing a little game that will cure what ails him.

If he's a senior who shoots 75, her husband already has a good putting stroke. Most likely what is wrong with his putting is not his stroke, but his touch.

This is what I suggested:

Her husband should take his putter and one ball and go round and round and round the putting green. Be sure to putt the ball into the cup on every hole.

I said her husband should gather a few of his senior friends who have the time and start a daily putting game. Play for a dime a hole—not enough money to make anyone nervous, but enough to keep score.

After a few weeks of this, her husband will be putting better than ever before in his life. And so will his friends.

I can't say this too often. You seniors—or Seasoned Citizens—grab your putter and one ball and head for that practice green.

Maybe you no longer hit the ball as far as the younger players. But there's not a reason in the world why you can't out-putt them.

A Story by Tom Kite

THERE WAS A TIME when I was probably fifteen or sixteen years old and had been working with Mr. Penick for about four years, and I had some success at one of those junior tournaments. I came back sort of full of myself.

Somehow I guess the word filtered back to Mr. Penick that I had gotten a little cocky.

(For thirty years he has been telling me to call him Harvey, but I just can't do it. It may be the only instruction he has ever given me that I can't follow. My respect for him is so deep that I may try to say "Harvey," but it comes out "Mr. Penick.")

Anyway, fresh from my junior triumph, I asked him to give me a lesson.

We went to the practice range, and he watched me hit some shots. We did the things we normally do.

As we finished, he started to walk away, and then he turned to me and said, "Tommy, you've been having a lot of success. You have been playing really well, and I am very proud of you. But I want you to remember this: You are what you are, not what you do."

Then he walked off.

Oh, man. It was like hitting me with a ton of bricks. It was like taking a two-by-four and slapping me up the side of my head.

There was no doubt in my mind what he meant.

I have tried to live by that statement ever since.

The True Way

I WAS WATCHING four of my University of Texas players getting ready to hit on the first tee one afternoon in the early spring.

They were discussing whether to play "winter" rules or "summer" rules.

"What do you think, Coach?"

I said, "Well, you boys can go play golf. Or else you can make up some other game and go play that, instead."

They understood my meaning.

In the game of golf, the ball is played as you find it.

The Bench

A FELLOW DROVE down to Austin from somewhere in Ohio to take a lesson in chipping.

I visited with him for a while and repeated the first fundamental of the chipping stroke—make sure your hands stay ahead of, or even with, the clubhead all the way through.

Then I brought out a bench from the locker room and placed it on the edge of the green.

"Now I want you to chip the ball so that it goes under the bench and rolls to the hole," I said. "I'll be back around to see you in half an hour."

When I came back, he was chipping like an expert.

"That's it," I said. "Now you're a good chipper."

He hauled his clubs to his car and drove back to Ohio.

A couple of nights later, Helen answered the telephone at home.

"Harvey, this is some men calling from a club in Ohio," she said. "They say their friend has turned into a wonderful chipper, but he's also become a horrible liar. They don't believe all you did was tell him to chip under a bench."

A Teacher's Guide

IN 1929, MY SIXTH YEAR as head pro, I pulled a pencil and a black ledger book out of a drawer in the golf shop and wrote for myself what could be called a guide to my thinking and behavior as a teacher and as a person.

I don't claim to be the creator of these principles. They are at least as old as the Bible. But I didn't write them in the black ledger book because I had learned them in Sunday school. I wrote them because I needed to use them in my everyday life.

This guide grew out of my experience as a caddie and shop manager and teacher. It is common sense. If it's so simple, why did I need to write it in the ledger in 1929?

In the midst of a lesson with a stubborn pupil that day, I found myself saying harshly, "I wish your brain and muscles were as coordinated as the clothes you're wearing!"

The look of hurt on the pupil's face caused me to apologize. I told him he was making progress and we would resume the lesson another day, by which time I would be a better teacher.

I walked into the golf shop, pulled out the ledger, and wrote the simple guide that I tried to follow for the rest of my life.

Like golf instruction, these principles are easy to learn, but useless unless they are put into action.

And like golf instruction, these principles are easy to forget. I need to read them every few days.

This is what I wrote:

o

Criticize yourself once in a while and see what you may be doing wrong. Never criticize others. It only stirs resentment. Speak no *ill* of anyone and *all* the good you know of everyone. Don't judge a person too soon. God waits until the end.

o

All people like to be important. Criticism from a teacher can kill the pupil's ambition to improve. Be anxious to praise and slow on fault-finding.

o

Nations and peoples also feel their importance. A top Eskimo feels superior to a Vanderbilt. Most people you meet feel superior to you in some way. Let them know you realize their importance, but avoid flattery.

o

Emerson said, "Everyone is my superior in some way." In that knowledge, I learn from them.

o

The best way to get pupils to do something is to get them to want to do it. Try to make the other person happy about doing something you suggest.

o

"Don't argue!" Even if you win, you usually lose your pupil's goodwill.

○

Don't tell pupils they are wrong. Most of us are prejudiced about ourselves. When we are wrong, we may admit it to ourselves—but not if someone is trying to force the "facts" down our throats.

○

I never know so much that I can't learn more.

○

Don't make direct contradictions to the sentiments of pupils combined with positive assertions of my own. Don't say, "Certainly, undoubtedly." Say, "I believe; I conceive; it appears at present; in some cases it might be right, but in the present case there seems to me some difference."

○

When I am at fault, simply say I am at fault and there is no excuse for it. I will do better next time, or at least I will change it.

○

Be friendly. Forget yourself. Stop thinking about "I." Listen to other people, keep interested in everyone else—caddies and members and all. Find out what they are doing and what they care about.

○

Try and remember names.

o

Try and talk plain.

o

A pro, or anyone, either goes forward or backward. What am I doing?

o

Try and be simple in living as well as in teaching or playing. The long odds are against us if we shoot the hard way.

o

Life consists of a lot of minor annoyances and few matters of real consequence.

o

We are frequently misjudged by our superiors, but never by our subordinates.

o

A stout heart usually accompanies a soft-spoken voice.

o

Finish one job well before starting another.

o

Listen to the kicks from anyone. You usually know the people and if they really have a kick coming.

○

Instead of doing what is right and best, we are influenced by associates. I must be an influence and example to members, caddies, and friends.

○

Always smile when you give anything, no matter how much it hurts. This means when giving service or anything else.

○

Be brave if you lose and meek if you win.

○

A good way to size up a person is to hear him say what he thinks it takes "guts" to do. A robber thinks it takes guts to do a daring job. A doctor thinks it takes guts to do a risky operation. A preacher probably believes it takes guts to tell his people to live according to the teachings of Jesus. The congregation will criticize him for it.

○

Teaching is a teacher's best advertisement. Caddies are good advertisers. They will watch you and copy you if they see that your teaching is good.

○

Practically all of the awkwardness and odd ways people have are an outgrowth of misunderstanding some of the few simple fundamentals.

○

I hear lots of shortcuts to par golf. But the only way to get there is with hard practice, sound style, and thought. I try to teach a pupil to swing the club correctly. The pupil must learn to hit the ball with that swing and get it in the hole.

○

Don't play too much golf or gamble at cards with the members. Call people *Mister* and *Mrs.* and make sure your assistants do the same. Stay away from the social angles of the club.

○

When I go to a doctor, all I ask is for him to have my interest at heart. I try to do that as a teacher. First of all, a teacher must try to understand what is going on in the pupil's mind. The teaching must be simple. Don't get technical. Put yourself in the pupil's place.

Musings on Rulings

MARK BROOKS, a University of Texas boy who now plays on the tour and is a member of Colonial Country Club in Fort Worth, stopped by to visit, and I was reminded of the time Mark was a victim of one of the silliest rules in golf.

I believe the rules of golf must be strictly obeyed. I believe the laws of the land should be obeyed, too, but that doesn't mean none of them should ever be changed.

Mark was getting ready to putt in a tournament. He marked his ball and rolled it across the green to his caddie to be cleaned. But the caddie missed the ball like a second baseman letting an easy grounder go between his legs. Mark's ball rolled off the green into a water hazard.

Mark removed his shoes and socks, rolled up his trousers, and waded into the water to look for his ball.

He found nine golf balls, but not a one of them was his.

Mark's ball was not lost, because he had it marked on the green. On the other hand, Mark's ball couldn't be played, because it was somewhere under the water.

The official called a two-stroke penalty on Mark, citing the rule that a player must finish the hole with the same ball he started with, unless his ball gets lost, of course—which is a penalty of one stroke and distance.

It was one of those times when common sense tells you one thing, but the law tells you something else.

At a National PGA Championship in Denver, a lady was sitting on a shooting stick behind a green, and an approach shot landed in her lap.

She looked shocked for a moment. Then she jumped up, and the ball rolled about ten yards closer to the hole. It was up to me to make the ruling. The pro who hit the shot was in contention.

The question was: Did the ball hit her, or did it come to rest in her lap? If it hit her and bounced off, the pro could play from near the hole.

My sympathy was with him. But I ruled the ball came to rest in her lap. He had to drop his ball where she had been sitting and was left with a tough downhill chip to face.

On the ninth hole of the same tournament, Arnold Palmer's approach shot rolled across the green and well into the fringe. Some spectators who were drinking and betting caught Arnold's ball and tossed it back onto the green.

The question was: Where should Arnold take his drop?

Joe Dey and I discussed it. Joe said since we hadn't seen the ball stop, we should let Arnold drop where Arnold thought it should be. I couldn't see any other way to rule, either.

At another hole, a pro was way out in the deep rough with a bunker 50 yards in front of him. The grass was knee high.

The rule is, you can part the grass with your hands or club while you are looking for your ball, but once the ball is found you cannot part the grass again.

The pro found his ball and was getting ready to hit. But at address he couldn't see the ball anymore, it was so far down in the grass.

I saw him bend over and sort of stir the grass with his fingers, hoping for a glimpse of his ball.

This is a two-stroke penalty. I looked at the poor pro standing in the deep grass with an impossible shot and bills to pay, and I kept my mouth shut.

Lo and behold, the pro dug that ball out of that deep grass with a mighty blow and it sailed over the bunker and carried onto the green. He had such a joyful look. I just smiled and walked away.

Wilmer's Woes

WILMER ALLISON, great tennis player and coach, was devoted to the game of golf.

Late one afternoon, we were playing and we came to a par five. Wilmer hit a good drive down the middle. He hit a nice second shot right up in front of the green, just a short pitch away.

Wilmer shanked the pitch shot.

He walked around behind the bunker to play his next

shot, and he shanked it again. Now he was almost in back of the green as he set up for another pitch shot.

Again he shanked it.

This put Wilmer to the left of the green. He took a couple of practice swings, set up for his pitch—and shanked it again.

Four shanks in a row took Wilmer on a complete circle of the green and placed him back in the middle of the fairway.

We were all laughing—all except Wilmer, I mean—as he pulled out his putter and banged the ball onto the putting surface.

"Well, after all, Wilmer, it is the shank of the evening," someone said when we reached the next tee.

You can imagine where Wilmer's drive went.

The Power of
Negative Thinking

DESPITE THAT LITTLE ADVENTURE, Wilmer Allison almost never lost a golf game, because he nearly always had it won by the time he left the first tee.

If you could beat Wilmer, he wouldn't play you. He would take you as his partner.

And all the way around, Wilmer would harp about his

terrible luck. To hear him tell it, he had the worst luck of anyone who ever played the game. Wilmer never got a good bounce or a prime lie. Every break went against him.

This was Wilmer's way of luring his opponents into a false sense of security, which often led them into a streak of bad breaks and misjudgments.

The truth was that underneath his complaining, Wilmer knew he was going to win. His negative thinking was just a trick.

I always told my players just to worry about their own games. If you listen to what your opponents say, you'll head down a lot of wrong roads.

The Champion

NOT ONLY DOES Mickey Wright have one of the best—many would argue that it is the *very* best—golf swings in history, she is one of the classiest people it has ever been my privilege to know as a friend and pupil.

When she was asked at age fifty-eight why she had chosen to live a quiet life rather than cashing in on her many titles and her Hall-of-Fame status, Mickey said:

"I have no interest in translating my name into a million dollars, or any amount. To me golf means one thing and always has: the pure pleasure I get from swinging a golf club."

Practice It First

WHEN DARRELL ROYAL was coaching our football team at the University of Texas, he wouldn't have called upon his boys to run a play that they had never practiced in a game.

I believe the golfer should never try to play a shot he hasn't practiced a good deal.

On a windy day, most average golfers will go out and try to hit a low ball into the wind, or a high ball with the wind, when in the course of regular events they never practice either of those shots.

The only time most average golfers try to hit a soft, high wedge over a bunker is when they are faced with this predicament during a round of golf. You don't see many average golfers out there practicing with their wedges.

Much better for you to learn different shots on the practice range rather than banging away at the same one hour after hour.

I do advise, however, that average golfers select one club, perhaps a 7-iron, and learn to love it like a sweetheart. Learn how far it goes. Learn to hit it high or low, to hook it or slice it.

An average golfer can build a decent game around one club.

Wrongheaded Husbands

ONE OF THE BIGGEST PROBLEMS with women golfers is their husbands.

A husband nearly always tells his wife she "raised up."

This unfortunate woman will try her best to "stay down." But she can't hit the ball from there. She will hit the ground in back of it, or her left arm will bend at impact.

The most common reason for raising up is consciously trying to stay down. You can't raise up unless you are down to begin with.

The woman should be thinking, "chin up, stand tall"—not "stay down."

It pains me to hear the terrible advice husbands constantly give their wives regarding golf.

For years, her husband loudly admonished Joan Whitworth, one of my favorite women pupils, to "keep your head still." He got her so locked up that I could hardly persuade her to make a free swing. Joan is a fine athlete, too. What a pity her husband, Harry, didn't keep his golfing wisdom to himself.

Children

I DON'T TRY to teach golf to children. What they need is someone who will guide their learning. Let them play, then help them when they want you to, or when you see something that demands a teacher's attention.

Crosshanders

THE FIRST TIME they pick up a golf club and swing it, most children do it crosshanded. A right-handed child will put the left hand below the right hand on the grip.

I believe the reason is that instinctively a child knows that to hit a ball with a golf club, the left arm must be straight at impact. Pick up a club and try a slow crosshanded swing and you will see what I mean.

For a righthander, there is no way the left arm can keep from being straight at impact in a crosshanded swing. The left arm will bend in the backswing, but it will straighten as it comes down.

In the orthodox golf swing, with the left hand above the right on the grip, the left arm can all too easily break down through impact. This is a common mistake of poor players.

Most children will begin to copy adults and give up the crosshanded swing early. But some just keep on swinging crosshanded.

For a couple of summers I escaped the Texas heat and enjoyed myself as guest instructor at Cherry Hills in Denver. My son, Tinsley, was an assistant at the Pine-hurst club across town. It was a very pleasant time for me.

At Cherry Hills I received a stipend for teaching that allowed me the freedom to spend as much time, or as little, as I thought each pupil needed. If I thought I had done all I could do for a pupil in ten minutes, I just moved on. On the other hand, I could spend all day with a pupil if I wished. This is my favorite way to teach.

I met a fine young assistant pro named Buddy Phillips at Cherry Hills. Buddy loved to teach, and he loved to practice. He would practice like a machine, scraping over one ball after another and hitting them down the range.

I used to take the club out of Buddy's hands every so often just to make him stop.

"Athletes in other sports take a time-out," I would tell him. "Go sit on your bag for a while."

Buddy's son, Tracy, was a three-year-old golf prodigy as a crosshanded swinger. Tracy hit the ball blindfolded, it didn't matter. He couldn't miss.

Once the great trick shot artist Paul Hahn said to Tracy, "Now, watch the ball."

Tracy hit the ball while looking down the fairway. He

thought Paul Hahn meant to watch the ball while it was in flight.

Buddy bent down and whispered, "Mr. Hahn means watch the ball on the tee."

We must be very careful what we say to children in a learning situation.

Buddy asked me what he should do about Tracy's crosshanded swing. I advised him to let Tracy keep swinging the way that felt right to him. When Tracy grew older and realized he needed more distance to play with his peers, he would change on his own.

At the age of six, Tracy got a disease that causes a softening of the right hipbone. For the next two and a half years, Tracy played golf standing on his left leg with his right leg in a sling.

He would go around the putting green chipping and putting and hopping on one leg hour after hour.

At age nine, with his hip disease abated, Tracy finally asked his dad if he should continue playing crosshanded.

Buddy picked up a sleeve of new Titleists and a sleeve of new Maxflis and walked out to the tee with his son.

Buddy said, "Hit three crosshanded and three orthodox, and we'll see which go the farthest."

The balls were longer with an orthodox swing, so Tracy changed over.

Except for chipping and putting. He continued to chip and putt crosshanded—which I would suggest anyone should try. The left wrist stays firm with a crosshanded chip or putt.

Another thing Tracy did as a youngster that I would

recommend is that he chipped and putted while looking at the hole, not at the ball.

This is a wonderful way to develop touch. You don't look at the basketball when you shoot a free throw, you look at the rim.

I mean, you should try looking at the hole in practice. But Tracy did it while playing, too.

At age fifteen, Tracy came to me for lessons. He was already a wonderful player and had one of the best short games I ever saw.

Tracy won the National Junior and the World Cup Junior and about eighty more junior tournaments.

Now Tracy is a teaching pro in Dallas—and a very good one, I would bet—and his dad, Buddy, is head pro at Cedar Ridge, a big, prosperous club in Tulsa.

The lesson for us all is, if you see children swinging golf clubs crosshanded, let them be. They're just doing what comes naturally.

The Left Arm

KEEPING THE LEFT arm straight at the top is not a requirement for a good swing.

But the left arm absolutely must be straight at impact.

The Secret of the Golf Swing

WHEN AUSTIN COUNTRY CLUB was located on Riverside
Drive, I was walking from the parking lot toward the
shop when I heard my name being screamed from the
direction of the practice area.

"Harvey! Harvey! I've got it! Eureka! I've found the
secret!"

It was a member I had been teaching off and on for
years with only fair success.

"I've found the secret of the golf swing, Harvey! I
can't believe it's so simple!"

I said, "Please let me in on it. What is the secret of the
golf swing?"

The member grew very solemn and owl-eyed with
excitement.

"The secret is that the golf swing is just like hitting a
ball with a stick!"

"Really?" I said, trying not to smile. I remembered the
famous teacher, Percy Boomer, who was told by a pupil,
"Percy, you teach it backwards. You say I should drive
like I putt. The truth is, I must putt like I drive."

My pupil said, "It's as clear as can be. Like the sun

coming up to light the darkness. I can forget technical stuff and just swing the club as if I were hitting a ball with a stick. That's all there is to it. I don't know why you pros should make such a mystery of it."

I said, "Well, now that you have learned the secret, I guess you have no more need for a teacher."

My pupil said, "Thanks, Harvey. That's big of you."

This pupil moved to a different city a few months later and never contacted me again. Once the secret was learned, I suppose it stuck.

Hit It Hard

VERY EARLY in our time together I try to get my pupils to hit the ball hard, even with the short irons.

I believe if you start off in the game hitting the ball easy, you generally will keep it up. Your muscles learn the slow pace. You will always lack distance.

Sometimes it takes longer to unlearn than it does to learn.

Brand-Name Aiming

GOLFERS ON ALL LEVELS have been taught the trick of lining up their putts and then placing their golf balls down with the brand name aligned in the direction the putt should go.

It seems to me this is vaguely illegal. You can't lay a club on the green to use as an alignment guide. You can't aim a putt at your caddie's foot if it indicates the line.

But I don't know how a rule against this practice would ever be enforced. And I think the brand-name alignment does little, if any, good. In fact, it might be more of a distraction than an aid.

I believe your mind should be on the cup and on your touch rather than on the brand name of your golf ball.

The brand-name alignment is supposed to relieve your mind so you can concentrate on distance, but I think it often works in reverse.

Also, a common thing for the average player is to kneel down and line up the brand name, then stand up and look down and get the visual illusion that the brand name is lined up wrong. This really confuses matters.

Most players on every level do pretty well at aiming their putts. It is the touch for distance that separates the good putter from the not so hot.

Slices and Hooks

WHEN I MEET a new pupil who hits a hook, I know I am in for an easy time of it. I may not need to spend more than ten minutes with this pupil.

But when my pupil is a slicer, we are facing problems that may seem insurmountable. If you are hitting a slice, you are not going to get any better as a player. The more you swing, the bigger your slice becomes.

I don't see how a habitual slicer could really have a true sensation of how the game is played.

The first thing I set out to teach a new pupil who slices is how to hit a hook.

This may take a while.

But once the slicer has learned to hook, I can cure the hook quickly.

A pupil recently wrote me, "I know this is an unanswerable question, but I'll ask it anyway: What can I do about my slice? What's the first thing to try to fix? What's the most likely cause? Is there any salvation for a poor soul like me?"

Sure there is. Another teacher sent me a slicer with a note that said, "Harvey, if you can cure this person's slice, you can raise the dead."

This is what we did:

First, we used a 7-iron and made sure the pupil had as

strong a grip as looked reasonable. We made the pupil's V's point pretty much toward the right shoulder. I say I like to see a three-knuckle grip. But I don't like to see a pupil always looking down and trying to count knuckles. Just aim the V's generally toward the right shoulder, which will give you a three-knuckle grip.

Second, we squared the pupil's feet, hips, and shoulders to the line of flight. We made certain the pupil was not subconsciously allowing for a slice. Allow for a slice, and you will hit one.

Third, we played baseball.

I mean, we stood at home plate and aligned the pupil squarely with the pitcher's mound and second base.

Then we hit the ball over the shortstop.

We rolled the left forearm, not the wrist, to hit the ball.

The reason we hit the ball over the shortstop is so the pupil would not try to hit from the inside out. We want the ball hit from inside to square to inside.

But don't think about why. Just square up to the pitcher's mound and second base, then hit the ball over the shortstop with a 7-iron.

The pupil who came to me with the note about raising the dead now has a big hook, but is happy with being in the left rough at last. For a lifelong slicer, the left rough seems like a wonderful place to be—for a while.

Pretty soon, we'll have to cure that hook.

Pressure

DURING MY THIRTY-THREE YEARS as golf coach at the University of Texas, not only did I rarely travel to an out-of-town match with my teams, I didn't walk the course with them when they were playing matches here in Austin.

Usually I would watch them tee off on the first hole and then I would see them pass through at the ninth, tenth, and eighteenth.

I remember one match when I hid in the locker room and peeped out the curtain to see if my captain sank a vital three-foot putt on the final hole. He made it, and when I went outside to congratulate him, he said, "I knew you were in there."

Traveling with the teams was out of the question, because I had my hands full as head pro at Austin Country Club. But why didn't I walk along and observe their home matches?

My thinking was that my presence would only increase the pressure that my players already felt.

We had a quarterback at Texas named Bobby Layne who thrived on pressure. With the crowd screaming and everybody going crazy, Coach Blair Cherry could clap him on the shoulder and say, "Bobby, go in there and get us a score." Bobby would respond with a tremendous effort that often was successful.

But imagine me grabbing one of my golfers by the arm and saying, "We're depending on you, kid. Step up there and make that ten-foot putt!"

I always asked basketball coaches what they said to players who faced a crucial free throw that would win or lose the game. That's the closest comparison I can think of to a crucial golf shot.

In golf there is nobody to block for you or catch a pass. Like the free-throw shooter, you are alone with your mind, your heart, and your muscles.

Most basketball coaches said they told their players, "Just be yourself." Now and then a coach would say he told them, "The whole game is on your shoulders. You've got to come through!"

The best answer I got was from coaches who said, "You must know your players well enough to know how pressure affects each one of them."

When Betsy Rawls was a student at the University of Texas—the university did not have a women's golf team in her days there—I asked her if I would be a better coach if my players were afraid of me, as if I were a priest or a military officer. Betsy didn't have a team to play for, but she was entering tournaments and training for the Hall of Fame.

Betsy is a brilliant person, a Phi Beta Kappa in physics. If she hadn't become a golf champion, she could have been at the top of any field she chose.

She thought a long time and said, "No, not in your case. Your players know you get up early in the morning and go to bed late at night thinking about us. We know you're always available for instruction. That's all we need."

Dave Williams was a very successful golf coach at the University of Houston. Dave didn't play golf or teach it, but he knew how to recruit good players and keep them on a fine competitive edge, even if turning up the pressure was his answer.

Some golfers play just as well or even better than normal when the pressure is hot, and some fall apart.

The reason I want children to hole out every putt—no gimmes—and have something at stake on every hole, even if it is something imaginary, is so they will grow up accustomed to making shots under pressure.

I have seen players who can be thrown off their games by the slightest thing. Even the greatest can get their nerves tuned so tightly that a simple matter upsets them. I remember a tournament where a spectator's shadow fell across the line of Tommy Bolt's putt. Tommy looked at the sky and cried, "Lord, how can a man be expected to make a putt in the dark?"

I'm not sure which P. G. Wodehouse story it was, but I always laugh when I think of one of the characters who was too distracted to hit his shot because butterflies in the adjoining meadow were creating such a hullabaloo.

The Erratics

MANY GOOD PLAYERS continue to fire and fall back from success on the professional tour because they seem incapable of putting good rounds back to back.

Champions must string four good rounds together, or at least three. But the players I call the Erratics are not champions, and their names soon disappear from the sports pages.

Each Erratic is an individual, to be sure, and there is no one explanation why they continue to follow a 68 with a 77.

I believe, however, if I were trying to make a living playing golf I would keep a diary.

In my diary I would note such things as, Did I go out to dinner? What did I eat? Who was I with? What did we talk about? Did I drink spirits? How much did I sleep, and how well?

How did I feel physically? Was I tired? Did I have a head cold? How did I feel emotionally? Was I upset about something? Was I being cranky about small things? Or was my mind clear and my heart serene? Was my energy high? Was it low?

I would note what score I shot that day, the number of putts, and general comments on the all-around condition of my game.

Probably I would fill out my diary the last thing before bed. One thing for certain, I would never skip a night of writing in my diary.

What good would a diary do me as a professional golfer?

I feel that by periodically studying my diary, I would see patterns emerge.

My diary might show, for example, that I played better on days after I had eaten spaghetti for dinner with a couple of amusing pals and then watched a funny movie on television before lights out.

It could show, as well, whether spaghetti, companionship, and comedy were a prelude to disaster for me on the golf course.

There is no predicting what the diary might show, which is why keeping the diary is important.

The diary is the only suggestion I could give to an Erratic.

You don't lose your swing between the ninth green and the tenth tee, and you don't lose your swing from one day to the next. If you think you do, something is going on that you don't understand.

A diary might explain it to you.

How to Stop
the Bleeding

ALL GOOD PLAYERS reach patches in the midst of rounds when their games go awry.

I'm not talking about the habitual Erratics. I mean consistent, good players who for no apparent reason start making a string of bogeys, maybe a double bogey or two. They call it "bleeding." They ask me, "How can I stop the bleeding?"

As I always say of good players, you don't lose your swing between the green and the next tee, or between the tee and the approach shot.

The bleeding may be caused by bad breaks, which you simply must cope with. You should make birdies with your good breaks, but your bad breaks must not be allowed to mess up your thinking and poison your attitude.

Leaving breaks out of it, what causes the bleeding is what is going on in your mind during that five or ten minutes between shots.

While walking from your drive to your approach, is your mind caught up in considering results? Are you thinking ahead to future holes? For example, perhaps you are thinking, "I'll knock this wedge stiff for a birdie, then par that long, hard hole, reach the 17th in two for a cinch birdie—and par on the final hole will pay me a great, big fat check!"

Not only are you living too far in the future to be playing a sharp game of golf, you have let the thought of gold enter your mind. There may be gold and riches awaiting you, but not if you have started dreaming about them. You reach your reward stroke by stroke. You must be mindful of each stroke as it is played. Golf is played in the present.

If you can wash your mind clean each time while walking to your next shot, you have the makings of a champion.

That's what I mean by taking dead aim. I mean clearing the mind of all thoughts except the thought of the target, so that the muscles are free to do the job.

A good player's muscles do what they are told to do if they are free to do it.

Now let's suppose you are struggling with getting your mind on the job at hand, but nothing helps. You just can't do it. You can't stop the bleeding. What do you do?

You take it to the Lord in prayer—that is my best answer.

The Dashing Demaret

AT OUR ORIGINAL Austin Country Club—the first of our three locations—the dashing young Jimmy Demaret walked into the shop one day and asked me to play a round with him.

"I'm working on something in my swing. Let's go see how I'm doing with it," he said.

In later years, as he went on to win three Masters championships, Jimmy became a little plump and was famous for his colorful style of dressing, which attracted many fans to the game.

But on the day I am speaking of, Jimmy was thin and wiry, with big, strong forearms and powerful hands. I had powerful hands myself, from years of grinding and buffing clubs, but I wasn't as strong as Jimmy by any means.

Jimmy also was one of the most handsome fellows ever born and had a quick wit that stood him well in the company of such wits as Bob Hope and Bing Crosby.

Even as a young man, my face had already begun to wrinkle from sun and wind and, I suppose, something in my genes. Jimmy used to say, "Harvey, I could pour a bucket of water on your head, and not a drop of it would reach the ground."

Anyhow, Jimmy and I set out for a round of golf on the original Austin Country Club course.

"What is it you are trying to do with your swing?" I asked him on the tee.

He said, "I am trying to keep my elbows out in front of me on my follow-through."

I watched his swing intently that day, but I didn't get to see it very often.

Jimmy shot 30-29—59.

Ever since, keeping the elbows out in front on the follow-through has been one of the things I emphasize in teaching.

Luck

WHEN TOMMY KITE chipped into the hole at the seventh for a birdie two on the last round of the U.S. Open at Pebble Beach, was it luck—or was it the perfectly struck shot?

Or was it so nearly the perfectly struck shot that it gave luck a chance to happen?

When I give encouragement to someone, I say, "Play well" instead of "Good luck."

In the Mind

MY OLD FRIEND Don Massengale arrived at the club looking dejected. He hadn't been playing well on the Senior Tour. I kidded around with him, saying I had to turn the sports page upside down to find his name, but he was not amused.

"Let me watch you hit a few," I said.

Don borrowed a 3-wood from a member on the range. Don was wearing slick-sole loafers and bifocals, and the place he chose to hit from gave him a downhill lie.

He stood there and banged 3-woods, one after the other, straight down the middle about 240 yards. He never came close to missing one, and I never offered a word of advice.

All I could say to him was, "Don, anybody who can hit the ball as I have just seen you hit it had better go back out there and keep playing. There's nothing in your swing that should cause you to be in a slump."

With good players like Don, problems are nearly always mental.

A simple thing to remember, but a hard thing to grasp and do, is this—if you want to change yourself, you must change how you think.

Fate Takes a Hand

IT WAS A CRISP MORNING in May, and the Southwest Conference golf championship was on the line.

As the University of Texas coach, I sent my four best players—Morris Williams, Jr., Marion Pfluger, Wesley Ellis, and Billy Penn—to Fort Worth to play undefeated TCU at one of the finest golf courses in the world, Colonial Country Club.

From its inception Colonial has been rated the top course in Texas, or very close to it. But in the days of this match I am about to describe, Colonial was even tougher than it is today. Storms and floods have destroyed many of Colonial's giant oaks, and architectural decisions have pulled some of the teeth that the original designer, my friend John Bredemus, put into the layout.

I am not diminishing the Colonial of today. It is a great course. But forty years ago—when Colonial was known as Hogan's Alley—it was tighter and harder than it is now.

My number-one player, Morris Williams, Jr., had lost only one match in his life. That was when Harvie Ward, the best amateur in the world for ten years, beat Morris 1-up in the 36-hole NCAA final in 1949.

Morris had beaten Billy Maxwell, Don January, Earl Stewart, Don Cherry, Joe Conrad, Buster Reed, and the

Cupit brothers, among others, during his brief career that was to be ended soon in a plane crash.

We needed to win at Colonial to assure Texas another SWC title. So I matched Morris against the TCU captain, a tall, slender, cocky sophomore named Dan Jenkins.

This Jenkins boy was not only a full-time student at TCU, he was also a full-time sports writer for *The Fort Worth Press*.

From the tips Colonial played more than 7,000 yards and looked twice as long. As a concession to the members, who were generous to allow college teams to compete there, the TCU and Texas squads started on the back nine first.

Morris had never seen Colonial, but he later told me that Jenkins, with whom he had become friendly, was nice enough to point out every danger and pitfall that Morris might have overlooked.

On the tee Jenkins would say, "You want to stay left here . . . a creek comes in over there . . . this next green is slick as a glacier."

No doubt Jenkins was trying to mess up Morris's mind. But that sort of needling never worked with Morris. With his pants cuffs turned up a couple of times, and a repeating upright swing, Morris almost never missed a fairway or green. When Morris had a 9-iron or wedge in his hand, he expected to hit it stiff. Morris played with incredible confidence, the kind that comes from knowing you'll have to be under par to beat him. Morris was grinning and friendly, almost apologetic about how good he was.

After 15 holes Williams and Jenkins were even par and level in the match.

Ben Hogan and Marvin Leonard, the mercantile king whose imagination and money built Colonial, drove up in a golf cart to watch them.

Morris was greatly impressed. He asked Dan, "Does Hogan follow you guys much?"

"Oh, sure, all the time," Jenkins said.

At Colonial's seventh hole—the 16th of their match—Jenkins pushed a 1-iron off the tee into the right rough behind some trees. Morris hit a 3-wood down the middle.

Jenkins had a shot if he could hook a high 6-iron over the trees and hit it far enough to reach the green. With Hogan watching, Jenkins hit perhaps the best shot he would ever hit in his life. The ball came to rest six inches from the cup for a cinch birdie. This birdie would have put Jenkins 1-up on Morris with two holes to play.

From back down the fairway, Morris pulled out a 7-iron, settled into that square stance of his—and hit the ball into the cup for an eagle!

Deeply shaken, Jenkins 3-putted the next hole and lost the match, 2-and-1.

Texas had won another championship. Morris shot a 68, two under par, the one and only time he ever saw Colonial.

One year later in the Southwest Conference Tournament—a medal event that was played to establish the individual champion—this same Jenkins kid 3-putted sixteen times in 72 holes to finish third behind Buddy Weaver of Rice and Wesley Ellis of Texas.

Over the years, I have come to know Dan Jenkins as a friend as well as a famous sportswriter and novelist.

I like to tell him, "Well, Dan, think how lucky you are. If Morris hadn't holed out that 7-iron, and if you had 3-putted only twelve times at the tournament, you might today be an assistant pro at Goat Hills."

Unfair to Ben

IT ANNOYS ME TO HEAR the television commentators talking about Ben Crenshaw being a wild driver who is always in the rough and has to save himself with miraculous putting.

It's not just because I love Ben like my own son, either.

Ben is indeed one of the best putters who ever lived, right at the top beside Horton Smith.

And it is true that he can get down in two from the parking lot.

But it is not true that he is a wild driver compared to some of the outstanding players among his peers. This is just one of those things that some television announcers say and some sportswriters like to write because it would seem to be a colorful trait.

If you would pair Ben in a tournament with Davis Love III and Fred Couples, for example, I would bet my five dollars that Ben would be in the fairway as often as any of them.

Made in Heaven

AFTER HIS LATEST birthday, Charlie Crenshaw, Ben's father, remarked that he might be nearing the end of his golfing habit.

"When your forward press is longer than your backswing, you've got to think about giving up the game," Charlie said.

But I know Charlie too well to believe he will ever quit. He'll be asking St. Peter to make him a match.

Chipping

MANY PUPILS COME to me with the notion that their chipping stroke should be the same as their putting stroke.

They have been taught that from a few feet off the green, chipping with, say, a 7-iron, they should hit the ball just exactly as if it were a long putt. Some even use their putting grips.

But chipping is not like putting.

Think of a chip shot as a little drive, and of a drive as a big chip shot.

To take your putting grip, you weaken your left hand and strengthen your right. The object of this is to keep the putter blade square to your line.

For a chip shot, use your regular grip. But place your hands toward the bottom of the handle. Play the ball in the center of your stance. Lean slightly more weight on your left foot. Make a backswing and forward swing of the same length, as if you were tossing the ball under-handed. And, of course, keep your hands ahead of, or even with, the clubhead all the way through the shot, including the follow-through.

If your ball is a few feet off the green and you want to use your putter—what we call the Texas Wedge—then by all means use your putting stroke to go with it.

But unless you have a putter in your hands, you don't want to stroke the ball like a putt.

One good practice for chipping is to put your golf bag down about eight feet in front of you and then hit chip shots that bounce off the bag. At first you may find yourself hitting the ball over the bag, because you are trying to help the ball into the air. Keep at it until your shots bounce off the bag. It's the same idea as chipping beneath a bench.

From the edge of the practice green, don't stand and chip at the same hole over and over. Aim for holes of different distances. Touch is what you are trying to develop.

Probably the most common mistake among average players is trying to chip with too much loft. It requires the touch of an artist to hit a chip shot with a wedge. The average player should get his ball on the ground and rolling as soon as possible. Chip with the least lofted club that will do the job.

A strong chipper and putter has a good chance to beat anybody any time. As I used to tell my university players, "If your opponent keeps getting down in two from off the green and beats you, don't think it's luck."

What Do You Look At?

WHAT DO YOU look at when you look at the ball?

If I looked at the back of the ball, I would hook it.

If I looked at the top of the ball, a thin shot would be the result.

If I looked at the inside rear quarter of the ball, I would have too much to think about.

When I look at you, do I look at your eyes? Your nose? Your mouth? No, I am aware of these features, but what I see is the whole you.

And that's what I think you should see when you look at a golf ball. Be aware of the whole ball, but not intent on any one part of it.

Telephone Lesson

SANDRA PALMER PHONED our home and asked Helen to ask me to help her with her follow-through.

I could hardly see her follow-through over the long-distance line, and it was difficult for Sandra to try to describe it to Helen, who tried to describe it to me.

Finally I said, "The follow-through is a result of what has gone before it. Ask Sandra what her problem is with striking the ball."

Helen said, "She says she leaves too many shots out to the right."

I said, "Tell her to toe in her club a little before she places her hands on the grip."

This is the same thing as strengthening her grip, which I couldn't do unless I could see her hands on the club.

It's just an aspirin, not a cure. I felt like a doctor of a bygone era, when a person would call with an ailment and the doctor would say, "Take an aspirin and phone me tomorrow."

But I know that toeing-in the club would straighten her shot, and that would have to affect her follow-through.

Still the Most Dreaded Shot

MY MAIL BRINGS many letters like this from a woman in Kansas City:

"Dear Harvey, I read your *Little Red Book* and gave special study to the chapter you call 'The Dreaded Four-Footer.'

"In my case, you could call it 'The Dreaded Three-Footer.' Or even 'The Dreaded Two-Footer.'

"The awful truth is that in our club wife-husband tournament last weekend, I had twenty-two 3-putts in 36 holes. I missed twelve putts of four feet or less.

"Harvey, I missed four putts of no more than one foot!

"And I was trying hard!

"I was doing exactly what you said to do on a short putt. I approached every putt from behind to see the line. I took one, two, or three practice strokes, concentrating on the line. Then I imitated my last practice stroke. I was careful not to look up and peek at the ball. I set my mind on stroking the putter on the sweet spot and on the line. I told myself, 'No negative thoughts.' I told myself, 'Forget the distance, just keep the putter blade square.'

"But they don't go in. I am putting worse than ever. My husband says I am crazy. What can I do?"

The woman's letter is a self-diagnosis.

She is thinking about the fundamentals while she is putting in a tournament.

The place to think about the fundamentals is on the practice green, over and over, hour after hour.

Your putting system must be automatic.

Many golfers become so involved in the process that they forget the goal—which is the bottom of the cup.

There are two good reasons why the three- or four-foot putt is the most dreaded shot in the game for so many average golfers once they get into some kind of tournament.

The most obvious reason is that average golfers never practice three- or four-foot putts. Oh, they will hit a couple before they tee off, but missing them may do more harm than good. I mean, how many average golfers do you see standing on the practice green for hours knocking in three-foot putts? The answer is: None. Only pros and top amateurs seriously practice three-footers.

The other reason, I think, is "gimmes." Many average players will practically get down on their knees and beg to be given a two-footer in a friendly game.

Much better to putt them all and not play under the illusion that two-footers are "good."

That's like thinking the banker will stamp your note "paid in full" if you are only a few dollars short.

Jack Did It

THE MODERN ALL-WEATHER, slip-on golf club grip was invented by Jack Burke, Sr., when he was the pro at Fort Worth's Glen Garden Country Club—where Ben Hogan and Byron Nelson were caddies.

Jack took a regular rubber hose, cut it the proper length, slapped some glue on the club shaft, slipped the hose on, and trimmed it into a grip.

I was playing golf with Jack the first time I ever saw his new grip, which was truly an innovation in the golf business.

Before then, it was hard work to put a good leather grip on a club. You had to wind strips of leather onto the handle just exactly right and then glue them tight. To remove one of those wound leather grips, you had to scrape and sand and file.

But with Burke's grip, you could pop it on or off in five minutes. It changed the lives of all golf pros.

The Downhill Lie

THE MOST FEARED FAIRWAY shot for the average golfer is the downhill lie.

A common mistake I see is that the player will try to stand up too straight.

The way to address the shot is with your body aligned on the same angle as the slope. For a right-handed player, this means your body will be slanted to the left.

Be sure to have enough weight on your left side to keep your balance.

Play the ball back in your stance. Swing the club with your hands and arms. Avoid the urge to raise up until your clubhead is through the ball.

Tension is a major wrecker of the shot off a downhill lie. Remember that your goal with this shot is not power, but a solid strike.

Haunted

MY CLOSE FRIEND Dick Metz, Wild Bill Mehlhorn, and I were paired at a tournament. Dick drew me aside as we were warming up.

He said, "I have to warn you, Harvey. Bill is so nervous about his putting that he will insist on hitting first on every green to get it out of the way."

Bill Mehlhorn won twenty pro tournaments, played on the Ryder Cup team and was a top teacher, but he was always haunted by the feeling that he was the worst putter in the world.

People ask me, "How is it possible for a person to win twenty pro tournaments and believe he is the worst putter in the world?" All I can answer is, "That's golf."

Dana X. Bible was the wildest hitter of the golf ball that I ever saw. He was a star player in football and baseball, and he won national championships as coach and athletic director at the University of Texas. But he couldn't shift his weight to his left side in his golf swing, no matter how many years of lessons I gave him. It seemed to be a total contradiction. This talented athlete could run for a touchdown or hit a home run, but to hit a golf shot he had to tee up the ball.

Of course, he didn't try to hide it. If you were playing with him for the first time, he would say, "I am going to tee up the ball whenever I want to, and you may feel free to do the same."

Our fairways in those days were scattered with worm casts, which D.X. used as tees when convenient. He insisted upon hitting up on the ball. Changing him was beyond my power.

I think people inherit quirky characteristics that may never show up except on a golf course.

In Bill Mehlhorn's case it was the contradiction of a superior golfer's being totally terrified of putting.

Hogan Whiffs It

IT WAS A CHARITY MATCH. Morris Williams, Jr., and Ed Hopkins were teamed against Ben Hogan and me.

With a large gallery around the first tee and people lining the fairway, we were waiting for Hogan. At last here he came, staggering a bit, a crooked grin on his face, his cap slightly aslant.

I could hear grasps from the crowd. "What's wrong with Hogan?" people whispered. "Why, it looks like he's drunk!"

Hogan fell to his knees trying to put his ball on the tee. He struggled to his feet, squinted down the fairway, rubbed his eyes, lurched backwards. Murmurs from the gallery grew louder.

Ben took a mighty swipe at his drive and missed it. He grunted. He waggled and knocked his ball backwards off the tee. A caddie replaced it. Hogan tried again and topped his drive about 50 yards.

Morris, Ed, and I hit decent drives. We marched down to Hogan's ball. Wobbling, Ben lashed at his ball and hit a big slice. His cap fell off. The caddie picked it up for him, and Hogan put his cap on sideways.

Finally we reached the green. Ben knocked his first putt some 20 feet past the hole. He was still away. His second putt again went 20 feet past the hole. The gallery was aghast. Staggering, Ben lined up his third putt—and somehow the ball dropped into the cup.

Retrieving the ball, Ben fell down again. I could see the dismay on the faces of the gallery.

Ben stood up, looked around at the people ringing the green, and broke into a big smile. He straightened his cap. He said to me, "Okay, pardner, it's up to you on this hole. I'll do better from now on."

Suddenly the gallery caught on. Everybody started laughing.

Hogan wasn't drunk. He was just putting on a clown act for the people. Bob Hope couldn't have done it better.

It's hard to believe for golf fans who have grown up watching the great Ben Hogan, stern and impassive, winning major championships, but when he was younger Hogan was a terrific entertainer and salesman with a wonderful sense of humor.

The rest of the way, Ben played that charity match as if it were the U.S. Open. The college boys beat us 1-up.

Few people remembered the result of the match, but everyone that day remembered Hogan on the first hole. They talked about it for years. It was a side of Ben that not many galleries ever had a chance to see.

Game of Honor

GOLF IS A GAME of honor. If you are playing any other way, you are not getting the fullest satisfaction from it.

Observing the customs of honor should be so deeply ingrained that it never occurs to you to play dishonorably.

There have been countless examples of players calling penalty shots on themselves for violations that no one else saw—and in some cases losing tournaments because of it.

During the third round of the Kemper Open in 1993, Tommy Kite was leading and was paired with Grant Waite of New Zealand.

Near the fourth green, Waite took a drop from a Ground Under Repair area. As Waite prepared to hit to the green, Tommy looked over and noticed Waite's heel was still inside the Ground Under Repair marker.

This was a tournament Tommy wanted very much to win. It was his first strong showing since a back injury in the spring. It would have been so easy to glance away and pretend he hadn't seen where Waite was standing.

That is, it would have been easy for some people. For Tommy Kite, it was not even a consideration.

"We don't need any penalties here," Tommy said, pointing out the location of the New Zealander's heel.

If Waite had hit that shot, it would have been a two-stroke penalty. The penalty would have put Tommy in the lead by three. But, as I said, Tommy never gave it a thought.

Tommy said, "It would be pretty chicken for me to stand by and watch a guy accidentally break a rule and then say, 'By the way, add two strokes.' That's not golf. That's other sports where guys are trying to get every advantage they can."

Waite won the tournament by one shot. Tommy finished second.

I think I'm more proud of Tommy for that tournament than I am for his U.S. Open victory. An Open champion is a winner on the golf course. A person of honor is a winner everywhere.

GOLF WORLD

The 'Golf' magazine

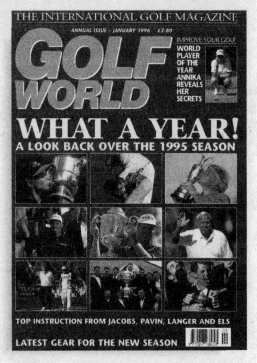